# A Comforting Word
## Poetry for Spiritual Enrichment

### by
### Alfrenia Gray

Brighter Day

Unless otherwise indicated, all Scripture quotations are taken from *The King James Version* of the Bible.

Direct quotations from the Bible appear in bold type.

A Comforting Word
ISBN 0-88144-214-3
Copyright © 2004 by
Alfrenia Gray
Tulsa OK

To

my husband Wesley,
God appointed loving and faithful head of
my life
A true source of strength and inspiration

To

Our children, Araba, Arrica, Wesley,
Aaron, Christian,
and Loyd

To

My niece, Petrina
All of whom are gifts from God and a
delight to train up in the way to go

## Acknowledgements

Special thanks to my son, Christian for typing much of the material for the manuscript. This was done in between work, school, play, and sleep time and always in a loving and willing manner.

Also a special thanks to my husband and children for lending me their time and their ears whenever I needed them to listen to a thought or give an opinion.

# Foreword

**Comfort ye, comfort ye my people, saith your God.** Isaiah 40:1 This scripture says it all. I believe God spoke this word to my wife many years ago. I've watched her over the years draw out of her soul to those that were afflicted and in bondage, to the broken hearted and oppressed, and to those that were heavy burdened.

God said, "I need someone who will allow Me to express myself through them with poetry that comforts, encourages, and enlightens." My wife said, "Here am I, send me." Yet it would not come easy. The sufferings she has had to endure, among which were the loss of three sisters and two brothers, all in their youthful years, would serve to bring her before God time and time again for a comforting word. It would also increase the burden she'd feel for others suffering with losses of all kind.

Many of the poems you'll read are taken from a chapter in my wife's life. They stand as a testimony of the deliverance and saving power of the Lord Jesus Christ.

It yet amazes me how God, deposited

Himself in my wife, and gave her this unique way to take rhyme and rhythm, and express Him at the tip of a pen. The anointing of God is felt while reading each poem, as many have testified.

This Christ centered work will cause you to reflect on your life, while the soothing truthful words will refresh your hopes and enable you to rise to new strengths toward conquering whatever that's before you. I believe that as you read this book with an open heart, the Spirit of God will draw you close and give you A COMFORTING WORD.

Wesley D. Gray
Husband, Pastor, Friend

# About the Author

Alfrenia Gray attended Lael University Bible College in 1984 under Dr. Anderson, where her life was profoundly changed through the teachings from the book of Isaiah, taught by Malcolm Smith. She currently ministers with her husband, Wesley Gray, founder of Words Of Wisdom ministries, where she is used to impart powerful words of deliverance into people lives, especially on marriage and family issues.

# Contents

# Preface

This book is a collection of poems written over a twenty-five year period, and is purposed to encourage and enlighten. Each poem was written in direct response to hearing the voice of God speak to me after praying for myself, or for someone else during some difficult times.

The reassuring and comforting voice of God many times was the sustaining power that enabled me to get through some seemingly impossible situations.

Being encouraged by my husband and others (as I would gladly share my poems with family and friends) this book slowly came together.

The Scriptural references used in this book, which came later, are all taken from the King James Version of the Holy Bible and were given to me by the Holy Spirit as I meditated quietly before Him.

I pray that the comfort of the Holy Spirit will enrich and uplift your heart as He blessed me over the years and anointed me to write this book.

## A Comforting Word

**John 14:16,18 And I will pray the Father, and he shall give you another Comforter... I will not leave you comfortless: I will come to you.**

Jesus spoke these words to His disciples as the time grew near that He would be crucified. Jesus, knowing that His time here on earth, in a physical body, was to end soon, spoke comforting words to encourage and strengthen His disciples for what was about to happen.

# He Is

*Love that creates order,*
*Wisdom that provides,*
*Understanding that realizes need,*
*Diligence that supplies.*
*Faith that builds courage,*
*Endurance that over comes,*
*Joy that gives peace,*
*Truth that makes us one.*

**John 14:6 I am the way, the truth, and the life: no man cometh to the Father, but by me.**

In this Scripture Jesus gives a quick but deep description of who He is. In expressing who He is, He goes to the heart of what we need to know about Him. For if we don't know Him as the way, the truth, and the life, then we don't know Him. Also, if we don't know Jesus we can't know the Father. Jesus said, "No man cometh to the Father but by me." He goes further to say that if you have Him then you also have the Father, because the Father is in Him and He is in the Father.

So, who is He? He is our salvation and more. He is the Living Word and the Son of the almighty God, the Creator of everything that is.

## Love

*Love is not just a promise*
*To honor and obey,*
*Nor remembering the words you spoke*
*On your wedding day.*

*Love is not your children,*
*Nor the friends that are so near,*
*Nor the words that were spoken,*
*To bring you inner cheer.*

*Love is that fire*
*That refuses to be put out,*
*Though difficulties arise,*
*That tends to bring doubt.*

*Love is within you,*
*An unquenchable fire,*
*That expresses it's self*
*Through will and desire.*

*And recognized at it's best,*
*By it's ability to stand sure,*
*For in the mist of all life's problems*
*True love will endure.*

**1 Corinthians 13:13 And now abideth faith, hope, charity, these three; but the greatest of these is charity.**

This Scripture and the preceding passage puts love to the test against some pretty powerful attributes. It would be good to be able to speak with the tongues of men and of angels, to prophesy and to understand all mysteries and all knowledge. It's good to have faith that moves mountains, and it's also good to give bountifully to the poor, except when there's an attempt to do these things without being motivated by love. When a person does these deeds without having genuine love for God and his neighbor we get something that's twisted, unreal and ineffective. Yes, it may have some small sense of the appearance of the real thing but is only a hollow act.

So I encourage you to seek God that His love may reside in you richly, stirring up hope and faith to accomplish all that he purposed you to do.

## Creation

*What great works I've seen,*
*Wrought by Thy hand.*
*You created the firmament,*
*And called forth the land.*

*All the stars in the sky,*
*You made them to be*
*An array of Thy glory,*
*Whose light shall not cease.*

*The waters and the air,*
*You made especially for man,*
*And then from the dust.*
*You formed him by hand.*

*This reveals Thy wisdom,*
*On which no one can expand,*
*And shows forth the power*
*Of the Master's plan.*

**Genesis 1:1 In the beginning God created...**

God created with His word, everything that is seen and unseen in heaven and in the earth. He has a plan, a time, and a purpose for everything He created. Everything was set into a time and season for its manifestation and or maturity according to God's plan.

There is nothing that was made that was not already made. The things that man call inventions are only the manifestations of their having acquired the knowledge to put into structure and use something God had already purposed to come into man's awareness--**there is no new thing under the sun**. Eccl 1:9

God is the Creator and He allows us to draw from His storehouse of existing plans, useful materials to produce and announce what's acceptable and well pleasing to Him.

## MARRIAGE

*A result of divine wisdom,*
*Having made a plan for two,*
*And calling each individual,*
*Without giving them a clue.*

*Yet in their yielding faithfulness*
*And honesty through love,*
*They hear the voice of God*
*Drawing them closer from above.*

*They meet with trust and faith in God*
*Both knowing they can not lose,*
*As a oneness begins to take place*
*Supernaturally their spirits fuse.*

*They share love above comparison,*
*To any worldly dream fulfilled,*
*For the world doesn't know the love that comes,*
*From being submissive to God's will.*

**2 Corinthians 6:14 Be ye not unequally yoked together with unbelievers: for what fellowship hath righteousness with unrighteousness? and what communion hath light with darkness?**

The Scripture warns us against contracting or teaming up with those whose beliefs and actions are inconsistent and unbecoming to the Gospel of the Lord Jesus Christ. It points out that in such a relationship it is necessary to be able to communicate and share with understanding the righteousness of God. In order to do this you'd have to be truly connected to God and each other.

Light and darkness cannot share the same space nor can they hold hands one with the other, there is a disconnection. Therefore in a contract where the two are to become one there needs to be an initial identification or a pre-qualifying in order to determine whether or not the two have what it takes in order to enter into such a contract. This is a must! And will save a lot of wasted time, heartache, and failure.

## Rain From Heaven

*Into each life God's rain must fall,*
*Timely sufficient and sure,*
*To provide nutrition and strength,*
*That every seed sown endure.*

*For when it rains provisions are made,*
*To protect from outward harm,*
*Yet within knowledge is gained,*
*And Godly character is formed.*

*Its hard to see how rain*
*Can produce any good in our life,*
*Perhaps in washes away all*
*The hatred, greed, and strife.*

**Matthew 5:45 ...and sendeth rain on the just and on the unjust.**

Rain throughout the Scripture has been known to serve for good or potential harm. The initial rain during the days of Noah in the book of Genesis 6:7,8 brought much harm to those who refused to heed the warnings by the man of God, Noah.

Elijah prayed that it might not rain, and it did not rain for a space of three and a half years and caused much harm to those suffering in the famine which followed. Then he prophesied that it would rain and there was a great rain which ended the drought (I Kings 18:45.)

The Scripture also speaks about the rains and the storms, which will come to destroy the house of that one whose house is not built on solid rock. The parable is signifying the end of those who hear the Word, but do not obey it. Matt. 7:24-27. And there are numerous other accounts of the affects of rain in the lives of people.

## He's Faithful to Forgive

*Here I am again Lord*
*Reaching out once more,*
*Asking Your forgiveness*
*As so many times before,*
*With tears of sorrow in my eyes*
*My heart is filled with pain,*
*I'm seeking You with all my heart*
*Your blessings I come to claim.*

*Here I am again Lord,*
*I find You here every time*
*With arms of love wide open*
*How wonderful, how sweet, how kind,*
*You wipe away all my tears*
*With tenderness and then,*
*Your joy, peace, and happiness*
*Fills my heart again.*

*Here I am again Lord,*
*It seems I heard this before*
*But the joy in coming back to You*
*You're the same as You were before.*

**1 John 1:9 If we confess our sins, He is faithful and just to forgive us our sins, and to cleanse us from all unrighteousness.**

All of us at one time or another, have felt like we'd blown it, like we have messed up self or something beyond repair. In the worst of these situations there is a sense of hopelessness with feelings of depression and/or despair.

The good news is that you're not the only one that has had or is experiencing these feelings. Many have and/or will find themselves with such feelings of hopelessness. There is a way out. All of us have sinned and fallen short of the glory of God. Yet what hinders some from receiving God's forgiveness is the denial that we've wronged Him or others. Scripture says, if we confess our sins He's faithful and just to forgive us and cleanse us from all unrighteousness.

So when you feel you've wronged someone don't run from Him rather run to Him. For, He is faithful to forgive.

## Continue in Faith

*Faith will last your whole life through,*
*As long as your hands find work to do,*
*That moves you toward your call and goal,*
*To receive the best your future holds.*

*Doubt is not so, it holds you back,*
*And keeps you under constant attack,*
*Of the things your heart once held dear,*
*As it leads you to despair and fear.*

*But remember God's word where all life*
*starts,*
*Let it strengthen and renew your heart.*
*As you recall the things God has done,*
*Your hope will build and your faith will*
*come,*

## James 2:20 Faith without works is dead?

This verse of Scripture goes beyond one's admission or confession of faith. Here there is a requirement that compels the believer to act. Verse 18 actually challenges the believer by saying **shew me thy faith without thy works, and I will shew thee my faith by my works.**

Yes, it is of utmost importance to read and hear the word to build faith, but the evidence that you have faith, that is that which justifies and under-girds your faith, is shown more by your actions. How do you conduct yourself after you believe and confess the Word of faith? Vs 21 says **was not Abraham our father justified by works, when he had offered Isaac his son upon the altar?**

So be encouraged to continue in whatever it is you believe God has said to you, do what He tells you to, and watch it come to pass.

## A FATHER IS

*A provider, protector, helper, and a friend,*
*A no nonsense counselor that will guide*
*you til the end.*

*He's a fixer, a builder, a sportsman and a*
*pro,*
*A tower of stability though he's always on*
*the go.*

*His strength is always there, as he heed's*
*your every call.*
*Though he pushes you to do your best, he*
*will never let you fall.*

*He teaches never to give up, tow the line*
*until the end,*
*That a winner never quits, and a quitter*
*never wins.*

*He is a man of honor, respectability and*
*love.*
*Endowed from the heavens, and the*
*Father God above.*

**Proverbs 4:4 Let thine heart retain my words: keep my commandments, and live.**

A father is the source of life and he is responsible to supply that which is needful to sustain and protect that life. He commands and requires respectful acknowledgement and timely execution of his commandments. He rewards and supports his children. He leads by example with integrity and love. By doing this he imparts his life into his children.

Therefore it is important to both hear the Word and to do it in order that the life of the Father might be in you.

## A Mother Is

*A teacher, advisor, a friend, and a guide,*
*she's understanding, full of wisdom, and always*
*on your side.*

*She always seems to know even though*
*she's not been told, what certain actions can*
*bring, and what your future holds.*

*She's a servant, a lawyer, a doctor, and a nurse,*
*someone who will listen and put your needs first.*

*Her standards are high, and her thoughts are deep.*
*Her word she will give, her promises she will keep.*

*A mother is kind, and has eyes that see through*
*what you are saying, to what's troubling you.*

*Her gentle approach with sincerity and love,*
*brings a message of hope, from our Father God*
*above.*

**Proverbs 31:10 Who can find a virtuous woman? for her price is far above rubies.**

A mother is precious, a woman of great value, and is over-refined. She has given herself to humility, discipline, and high standards. She is organized, wise, and is moved by righteousness and kindness. She yields herself to assure that all in her house is well cared for. She oversees every aspect of her house in order that things run smoothly and without interruption. She teaches her children and anticipates their every need. Her husband lacks nothing as she respectfully and lovingly submits herself to him. She is blessed, for she is a woman of God.

## Don't Gamble with Life

*Looking to find a place of desire,*
*I hurried on my way.*
*Fixed in my mind was the game of life,*
*Yet no one wanted to play.*

*Each time I'd try to win,*
*The odds I would got small.*
*No one would tell me the stakes were high,*
*Nor that the winner would take all.*

*I came real close to winning this time,*
*After putting up all the cost.*
*But before I knew it the game was played,*
*And the hopes I had were lost.*

**Romans 6:23 For the wages of sin is death; but the gift of God is eternal life through Jesus Christ our Lord.**

The word death here is defined as eternal separation from God. The soul of man will spend eternity apart from God, which is death or with God which is life. The Scripture tells us that in order to spend eternity with God we must accept by faith that Jesus is the Son of God and that He died on the cross and was raised from the dead. After believing this truth we must submit ourselves to obedience of the Word of God throughout our time here on the earth. It also teaches us that to disobey God or to not submit ourselves to God's Word or to go about seeking our own desires would entangle us in all manner of sin. Therefore we would partake of death, which is eternal separation from God.

God is Holy and righteous and cannot dwell with sin, but He has made a way for us to repent of our sin and receive His salvation through Jesus Christ

## Mercy

*I'm present in every trial of life,*
*Over seeing the cause and weighing the*
*price.*
*Undergirding that one who without me*
*would fall*
*And answering promptly as I hear Him*
*call.*

*I'm needed more than it could ever be*
*known,*
*For the penalties of error are severely*
*shown,*
*And without me nowhere might one be*
*found,*
*But in the clutches of torment and hell-*
*ward bound.*

*I rest in the bosom of all who love peace,*
*I ride boldly on the waves where rage dare*
*not cease,*
*Until in victory I deliver and that without*
*pay,*
*One calling have mercy, have mercy I pray.*

**Psalm 136:23 Who remembered us in our low estate: for His mercy endureth for ever.**

Thank God for His mercy! Thank God for His mercy! The mercy of God is His unmerited favor toward man. It's God's intervention to grant leniency based on no argument of justification. He says in His word "I will have mercy on whom I will." Yet we also know from His word that He is no respecter of person. This is a great mystery, it's mind boggling, how can there be mercy toward one and not the other and yet there be no respecter of person? It's God's doing and it is marvelous in our sight. We know that His thoughts are higher than ours and His ways are higher than our ways.

All of us have tasted of God's mercy in that while we were yet sinners God sent His Son into the world to die for us all. It's not His will that any of us should perish but that the world through Christ Jesus might be saved.

## A Prayer for Endurance

*Lord prepare my heart for life's events,*
*And my mind to understand,*
*Help me always remember that,*
*All power is in Thy hand.*

*Add to me strength dear Lord,*
*When weakness draws me close,*
*Make me ever aware of You,*
*And the things that I need most.*

*And when in time I find myself,*
*Thinking times are just too tough,*
*Let me hear your voice inside me,*
*Whispering softly don't give up.*

**Psalm 27:13,14 I had fainted, unless I had believed to see the goodness of the Lord in the land of the living. Wait on the Lord: be of good courage, and He shall strengthen thine heart: wait, I say, on the Lord.**

The battles, trials, and tribulations that pursue the people of God are many. Sometimes you're barely out of one before another attack comes. Sometime a number of attacks occur at the same time and you might think to give up. Yet deep within you know that you can go to God for strength when you need it, and that's what keeps you going. Asking for strength to overcome situations through increased knowledge, or for your enemies to be scattered, or for provisions that you might have need of, many times you'll find that He's waiting just to give you the answer.

To paraphrase, David said he would have given up in the mist of the hardships he was facing, except he couldn't let go his faith. God had brought him out of too many things, so he expected God to come and show him good, not when he get to heaven, but while he was alive here in the earth.

So don't you give up. God is no respecter of persons, what He's done for one He'll do for another. Call upon Him and wait patiently for His answer, **wait, I say, on the Lord.**

## My Ideal Place to Be

*Is like a comfortable chair*
*In view of the most perfect sunrise*
*On a day full of hope and cheer.*
*It's like a stroll along the ocean*
*With one which your heart holds dear.*

*Is like receiving the gift you've so long*
*hoped for*
*But never thought you would receive,*
*Or dreams of participating*
*In something so full of joy*
*That your mind just cannot believe.*

*My Ideal place to be*
*If in mere words I'm allowed to say*
*Is in communion with my God,*
*Hearing Him answer as I pray,*
*With words to help me make the right*
*choice*
*Within the sound of the Father's voice.*

**John 10:27 My sheep hear my voice, and I know them, and they follow me.**

Understanding your relationship to Jesus in the likeness of a sheep would be to see yourself as being totally dependent upon Him. We, like sheep, are totally dependent upon Him. Scripture says without Him we can do nothing. Sheep are meek and timid, and lack the ability to care for themselves, and will go into harms way without the leadership and guidance of the shepherd.

Staying within the sound of the shepherd's voice is imperative for the sheep. The sheep must also be able to discern the shepherd's voice. This is why the shepherd takes up a loving and very personal way with the sheep early on in order that the sheep begin to know the shepherd. Also during the first few days of the sheep's life the shepherd names each sheep and throughout the day He calls each one by name to keep them in safe relationship unto himself.

The voice of the Good Shepherd even our Lord and Savior, Jesus Christ, is described as a still small voice. In another place in Scripture, His voice is described as the sound of many waters. His voice has perfect timing. It's peaceable, persistent, comforting

41

and never disagrees with His word.

Being where I can hear His voice assures me that He's near, that He's watching over me, and that all is well. I take comfort in that.

### Quiet Time

*In the stillness of the moment*
*My heart began to hope,*
*My mind began to listen,*
*My spirit began to float,*
*Right out of my normal thinking*
*Came thoughts I dare not speak,*
*And visions much too precious*
*With goals much too steep.*
*Yet I knew that I was able*
*To wander as I will*
*For in quiet times I'm on the move*
*While my busy self stands still.*

**Psalm 1:2 And in His law doth he meditate day and night.**

There is so much hustle and bustle in our lives today that finding time to reflect on where we are and where we're going is near to nil.

Giving ourselves to setting goals and approaches to acquire or accomplish a desired hope or dream is just not happening. Therefore when our actions or lack thereof catch up with us it can produce anxiety, depression, and/or all manner of self-destructive behavior.

We need some quiet time. We need a place away from all distractions where we can be alone to meditate on God's Word. We need to get to a place where we can hear His voice. We need to be reminded of His plan, purpose, and provision for our lives, which will enable us to get back on track with accomplishing His will in our lives. We need some quiet time.

## The Walk of Life

*If you value your walk in life,*
*Then you must watch and pray,*
*Remember the evils of life*
*Are sufficient to each day.*

*Except your hope be sure,*
*You'll always walk alone,*
*In Christ all things are pure,*
*There's no way you can go wrong.*

*Now some seek silver, others seek gold*
*To purchase many things,*
*Those who's life the Savior holds*
*Want only what His love brings.*

*A place of joy and peace*
*And the Holy Spirit within,*
*A life where sin has ceased,*
*And true life in Christ begins.*

**Matthew 26:41 Watch and pray, that ye enter not into temptation.**

The Scripture here points out how easy it is for us to allow our flesh to find it's place of comfort when we really should be waging spiritual warfare. An old Bible teacher of mine said something I've never forgotten. She said the world is slowly rocking the church to sleep.

We are becoming so comfortable with that which satisfies the flesh that we are grossly neglecting the things of God. We seem to have forgotten that there are even such things as evil or satanic forces in this world.

The warning here is to watch and pray that you don't become overtaken by fleshly pleasures of this world to where you lose the spiritual battle and fall victim to the strategies of the evil one. I encourage you to watch and pray.

## Laying Aside Faithless Errors

*It's easy to make an error*
*In our effort to do what's right,*
*Especially when our steps*
*Are not guided by His light.*

*We go up when we should stay down,*
*We go in when we should stay out,*
*It's no wonder the things we do*
*Are a result of things we doubt.*

*Hands off the situation,*
*Lay aside your thoughts for His.*
*Trust in God with all your heart,*
*And accept His perfect will.*

*He'll guide you through life's problems,*
*Making straight every crooked place,*
*Giving strength to endure every trial,*
*With His joy upon your face.*

**2 Corinthians 5:7 For we walk by faith, not by sight.**

I hesitate to think where we might be if we didn't have faith to believe beyond what we can see. Scripture says He's given every man the measure of faith. Faith in God enables us to reach into the invisible realm and bring into existence things unseen. You may not be able to see how certain things might occur, but through faith we can believe and call those things that be not as though they were.

Heb. 11:1 says **faith is the substance of things hoped for,** Rom. 8:24 says **hope that is seen is not hope.** So even though you don't see everything, you still must allow His Word to guide you in order to lay hold of His promises and to see your hopes and dreams come to pass by faith.

## Watch for Signs of Wisdom

*There's a flow of busy people*
*passing everyday,*
*They never seem to notice*
*Signs of wisdom on their way.*

*Wisdom points the right direction*
*With one way to joy and peace,*
*But the flow of busy people*
*Headed wrong just doesn't cease.*

*Their way is loud and noisy,*
*With laughter being loud and clear,*
*But underneath the smiling faces,*
*There's a terrible dread and fear.*

*They hide their pain and sorrow,*
*How could they ever admit it's true,*
*That the road they've chosen to follow*
*Has no sign of peace in view.*

**Matthew 7:13 Enter ye in at the strait gate: for wide is the gate, and broad is the way, that leadeth to destruction, and many there be which go in thereat.**

It's amazing how many people that are extremely knowledgeable yet will not receive the wisdom or godly advice. Many of these confess to be saved, Yet when you look closely you begin to see signs of decay and destruction in their lives.

Now these people are not to be judged by us, however Scripture says in Gal. 6:1, **if a man be overtaken in a fault restore such an one in the spirit of meekness considering thyself lest thou also be tempted.** Many times even a Christian will not hear words of reproof and restoration. If Christians reject correction how much more will non-Christians reject God's wisdom?

Scripture says there is a way that seemeth right to a man. That which appeals to the eye and the desire of a man many times will lead to destruction.

The majority of the world is saying, "if it feels good do it" but they don't see the consequences until it's too late. Following the crowd can have detrimental results. But in the multitude of counselors there is safety. **The fear of God is the beginning of wisdom.** Psalm 111:10

## Fear Not

*Fear not My child and be of good cheer,*
*I've charged My angels to encamp around*
*here,*
*Everywhere you go, and even where you*
*dwell,*
*My angels are watching that all may go*
*well.*

*Fear not My child and lift up your eyes,*
*Your strength and power within Me lies,*
*Enough to defeat every threat you see,*
*And bruise the head of your enemy.*

*For in Me there is rest, and no room for*
*doubt,*
*No thoughts of defeat can linger about,*
*So rejoice in Me for I've delivered to you,*
*The words of life to carry you through.*

**Psalm 91:11 For He shall give His angels charge over thee, to keep thee in all thy ways.**

The Word of God speaks about an innumerable amount of angels that have their orders to keep watch over the lives of the children of God, in order to prevent them from meeting with harm. They're on assignment to stay around, live near, support, protect, provide, and fight for those whose lives are governed by the Word of God.

So you don't have to fear threats of impending danger of disease, famine, war, loss of jobs or any other thing. Through faith in God and obedience to His word we are more than conquers through Him that loved us and gave Himself for us.

## He's Faithful

*He's faithful isn't He?*
*He did just what he said,*
*When all hope seemed lost,*
*He raised Jesus from the dead.*
*And made Him the way,*
*So you and I can receive,*
*The promises of God,*
*To all that believe.*

*He didn't come to show off,*
*But with compassion and love,*
*To invite us all,*
*To His home up above,*
*That we might know true life,*
*And more abundantly,*
*Serve Him with love,*
*Through all eternity.*

**1 Thessalonians 5:24 Faithful is he that calleth you, who also will do it.**

As we study the Word of God and hear the testimonies of faithful men of God, and as we witness His interventions in our lives, more and more we can say He is faithful. Sometimes our faith doesn't hold out, yet He abides faithful.

We see through out Scripture how God watches over His Word to perform it. If He spoke it He will bring it to pass, and if He purposed it He will also do it. God will make His Word good.

You'll find through out Scripture how that God said it and it came to pass. He said it and it came to pass. He has said some things to you, and regardless how it looks, regardless of your age, or how much it will cost, God will bring it to pass. He's faithful.

### He Will Bring You Through

*When knowledge fails to correct me,*
*When I do what I think is right,*
*When life seem to forget me,*
*Hopes and dreams being far from sight.*

*My heart won't let me settle,*
*Or think I can not win,*
*And though I've come near to giving up,*
*I yet get going again.*

*I remember things weren't so easy,*
*When I first heard God's call,*
*And though there have been trying times,*
*He's brought me through them all.*

**Daniel 3:17 Our God whom we serve is able to deliver us from the burning fiery furnace, and He will deliver us.**

Every work of God is going to be tried by fire, to see what sort it is. There will come a time when things you've learned will be put to the test. You'll have to deliver on whether or not He really is Lord of your life. That is, you'll have to either sell out to Jesus or sell out to the world. This was the case of the three Hebrew boys. However they had already made their decision to live for God and were willing to face the fire rather than deny their relationship to God. They knew that God was well able to do all that they had learned of Him.

How about you? What is it that you're facing? What is the enemy threatening you with in order to get you to stop serving God? Whatever it is God is able to bring you through it. To choose not to serve Him would be the true failure or loss in your life. So whatever is before you, you can say like the three Hebrew boys, the God whom we serve is able to deliver us from the fiery furnace, and He will.

### The Joy Returned

*The joy returned to my heart,*
*Where sadness once had dwelt,*
*It swept out all the crevices,*
*And raise a purple sail.*

*It began a new mapped out journey,*
*As wisdom order it aright,*
*To sail the coast of love and peace,*
*From morning until night.*

*What joy it is to serve Him,*
*Through obedience to His word,*
*And sing the praises of deliverance,*
*To all who haven't heard.*

## Psalm 51:12 Restore unto me the joy of thy salvation.

Nothing takes away the joy in a life like the experiences of not being able to get problems resolved favorably or of having your hopes and dreams cut off.

The Bible says the way of the transgressor is hard. That word hard means not easy, fatiguing, severe, difficult to endure or demanding great physical or mental effort. This can produce lots of sorrow and sadness of heart.

Jesus' presence in our life took away the heaviness and burdens we'd been experiencing. His interventions in our life allowed us to receive the beauty of His goodness on the other side of our every problem. That's joy! Just knowing that you don't have to go through anything alone when you have the Lord in your life is joy.

It's important to continue in the things of God and to obey His word if we're to experience His joy. If you're walking in disobedience to God and have not started experiencing hard time yet, just wait, because it's coming. You may need to confess some things to God now and receive His forgiveness. Scripture says draw nigh to God and He'll draw nigh to you. Receive His presence in your life through obedience to His Word and His joy will return to you also.

### Did You Ever Wonder Why?

*Did you ever wonder*
*Why the sky's so far away,*
*Yet the clouds cast shadows*
*In our lives each day?*

*Why the sun can't brighten*
*The gloom that's in a heart,*
*Why a smile builds hope*
*And a frown takes it apart?*

*Did you ever wonder*
*Why a baby learns so fast,*
*And an elder can't remember*
*Things learned in the past?*

*Why technology is growing*
*And still man doesn't know*
*That the answers are all in Christ,*
*The gift of God who loves us so?*

## Job Chapters 38-41

Regardless of the amount of knowledge man may acquire, he will always have many questions that go unanswered. In these chapters, Job is hit by God with a barrage of questions that boggled his mind and caused him to see the awesomeness of God.

It's important to look beyond your self and really seek to know Him. There is Someone in control of what's going on in this world. The world would have you think that a non-sensical occurrence took place and brought about all the intelligible events responsible for the necessary materials and life in this earth.

As you seek answers to know the truth about how this world and man came to be, I pray you will dare to know God and the Lord Jesus Christ in the pardon of your sins. For in this you will find the answers and your life will never be the same again.

## What is Faith?

*The sensing of His presence*
*After hoping He'd be there,*
*And resting in His love,*
*When it seems no one cares*

*Drawing on His strength*
*When all effort within has ceased,*
*And rising up with joy,*
*Refusing to loose your peace.*

*It's knowing you can't lose*
*When everything says you've lost,*
*And banking on His shed blood*
*As sufficient for all cost.*

*It's getting up each morning*
*And looking trouble in the face,*
*With the surety of His presence,*
*His love, His power, and His grace.*

**Hebrews 11:1 Now faith is the substance of things hoped for, the evidence of things not seen.**

Faith is that which is produced through hope and trust in God. It's trusting in His ability to bring to pass or do what His Word says. But how can you trust in someone in whom you don't even know?

Your biggest challenge then is getting to know Him. By reading and obeying God's Word, you'll get to know God well, because He and His Word are one. As you draw knowledge and strength from the testimonies of the prophets and the saints of old your faith will increase. Yes, I said increase, because He's given every man the measure of faith. Also you'll then be able to recall God's faithfulness to you in past events in your life. So what is faith? Faith is knowing Him.

## Words

*Words are spoken with intent to convey,*
*Images and thoughts of the mind,*
*They open and shut doors of insight,*
*They create, reflect, and shine.*

*They answer all life's problems,*
*Giving comfort, encouragement, and love,*
*They give faith and understanding,*
*Drawn from knowledge up above.*

*Words can reveal the truth,*
*And they know right from wrong,*
*They can point the way to destruction,*
*Or direct you to God's throne.*

*They are stored within earthen vessels,*
*Yielding themselves as they will,*
*To proclaim a message of hope,*
*Upon which salvation is built.*

**Romans 10:9 That if thou shall confess with thy mouth the Lord Jesus, and shall believe in thine heart that God hath raised Him from the dead, thou shalt be saved.**

Words are more important than many may know. Scripture says in Heb 11:3 that **through faith we understand that the worlds were framed by the word of God, so that things which are seen, were not made of things which do appear.** We should be able to hang our hats on this Scripture. This Scripture plainly says that you don't have to see it for it to come to pass. In fact if you're walking in true faith you won't see it.

The words which we speak through faith in God, and according to His will, are taken by the Spirit of God and in due season will produce the evidence of what we've been hoping for.

However this can work the opposite also as the enemy of God is waiting to catch you saying some negative and/or destructive words in faith that he may work to bring about some evil event in your life. David asked God to put a watch over his mouth, to keep him from sinning against God.

Confessing things which are in accordance with the Word of God are important, for those confessions God will work to our salvation.

### Rejection Is

*Returning to the beginning,*
*Erasing things of the past,*
*Joining the team that's winning,*
*Even when you get there last.*

*Counting all your blessings*
*Til the simple ones are great,*
*Ignoring all negative thoughts*
*On which you build*
*Nothing less than faith.*

**Proverbs 24:16 For a just man falleth seven times, and riseth up again.**

Rejection doesn't define who you are. To be disallowed or not accepted does not determine your value. Rejection is an opportunity for you to look within. It's a defining moment in your life when taken the right way. Many times when others reject us we take it as a failure and we seriously consider that maybe we don't have the " right stuff." Many are so in to measuring themselves by the opinions of others that they may never come to know their true value.

God thought you to be so valuable that He gave His only begotten Son that He might receive you unto Himself, and has built within His plan for you a way up and out if at any time you find yourself in a low estate. A righteous man can't be held down.

So rejection is another opportunity for you to allow God to demonstrate His ability to raise you up and present you as a valued child of the living God.

### Hidden Treasures

*Crouched in every span of life,*
*And beyond that which we know,*
*Are the unction's of the Spirit,*
*Which challenges us to grow.*

*When exploring thoughts for the cause of*
*man,*
*And examining how we might help,*
*We're reaching deep into the spirit realm,*
*Where the riches of God are kept.*

*And though we enter in alone,*
*Rather if we make it through,*
*The act of going in itself*
*Will make a treasure of me and you.*

### Hebrews 5:12-14

These Scriptures express how God expects us to move pass the initial exciting dancing and shouting period of our new birth to a place of maturity. Now there's nothing wrong with shouting and even dancing when truly motivated by the Spirit of God. God wants to bring us to a place of maturity defined as, a time when we should be able to teach others what it is that they're shouting about.

Scripture also talks about a babe in Christ as a worldly, youthful, and fleshly time whereby we conduct ourselves outside of spiritual knowledge. Yet as we yield ourselves to the obedience of the Word of God it enables us to not only discern right from wrong, but we are able to bless others with the increased knowledge we will acquire and with the gifts God's given us.

I pray that the treasures within you might be discovered as you obey God's Word to the glory of God.

## A Prayer of Submission

*He to whom it is my soul must bear,*
*When the world around seems so unfair*
*When life's problems, I now declare,*
*I've no strength to endure.*

*Yet my soul within won't die,*
*My inner man to Thee Lord cry,*
*To You my problems I now confide,*
*For through You my help is sure.*

*Come heal me Lord, come make me whole.*
*I yield my life to Thy control.*
*Keep me where I need to be,*
*I yield my life to Thee.*

**Romans 10:3 For they being ignorant of God's righteousness, and going about to establish their own righteousness, have not submitted themselves unto the righteousness of God.**

It would be wonderful if we would choose to serve God just because we received the invitation to do so. Yet those of us that serve God know that it did not happen that way. Many of us through much sorrow, heartaches, and hardships reached a place of despair causing us to cry out to God for help. Many times it's in such a state that we will begin acknowledge our need for God's intervention in our lives. Too often we go for long periods of time thinking we can make it without Him. God is our help, without Him we can do nothing.

We lack so much knowledge about what's needed to sustain life, that much of what we think is good, is self-destructive. We need the God that knows what we have need of even the creator and maker of our soul. We need to submit ourselves to God almighty in sincerity and receive His righteousness that we may have the life that only He gives.

## Running for Jesus

*I'll run this race many have lost,*
*Because my soul know it's cost,*
*Looking ahead I'll forget the past,*
*My heart has found victory at last.*

*No it wasn't I that made it so,*
*Nor in my strength will I go,*
*But He who set God's children free,*
*Sent words of life to you and me.*

*As I look to one so powerful and strong,*
*There's nothing in this race I can do wrong,*
*When the race has run He'll cause me to rise,*
*In heaven He'll then present me my prize.*

*That's why I'll run this race many have lost,*
*Because my soul know it's cost,*
*Looking ahead I'll forget the past,*
*My heart has found victory, victory at last.*

**Matthew 10:22 but he that endureth to the end shall be saved.**

Here Jesus is finishing up on a few warnings to the disciples designed to prepare them for their life long experiences as Christians. He's pointing out how that they're going to meet with some events in their lives that may cause them to want to give up. He says to them that if you endure these things you'll be home free. You shall be saved.

Scripture also says that in the last days perilous times are coming upon the earth and that there is going to be a falling away from the things of God. Yet Jesus says in Luke 21:28 that when we see these things coming to pass to look up for our redemption draws nigh. We're to know that we can make it, that it won't be long now. We're already closer than when we first began, so finish the race and enter into His rest. Because the only way to lose this race is for us to give up.

## Love the Lord with All Your Heart

*It's not enough to hear His voice calling*
*from afar,*
*Nor to know that He is willing to meet*
*you where you are.*
*It's not enough to go to church, to hear*
*God's Word and pray,*
*If there's no intent in your heart to*
*practice what it say.*

*It's not enough to decide that you no*
*more will sin,*
*For in order to see this come to pass, you*
*must be born again,*
*It's not enough to understand, all things*
*are possible if you believe,*
*If you refuse the power of God, which*
*enables you to achieve.*

*But if you receive all God's Word,*
*And to Him always be true,*
*Love the Lord with all your heart,*
*And He will see you through.*

**Matthew 22:37 Thou shalt love the Lord thy God with all thy heart, and with all thy soul, and with all thy mind.**

This Scripture calls for complete surrender to God in love. It reveals that there is no set of rules and regulations where by man can acquire degree of service that will give him access to God or heaven.

The fulfillment of the law is love. Therefore, man shall be governed by his own heart, soul, and mind, which should be filled with the love of God. He doesn't need a schoolmaster, law enforcer, or guard, only sincere complete love towards God.

## The Sound of Rain

*I hear the rain,*
*Speaking softly of the time,*
*Crowding the corridors of my mind,*
*I hear the rain.*

*I hear the rain,*
*Never as clear as today.*
*Saying all is okay,*
*Yes, I hear the rain,*

*Something good is sure to come,*
*Something new something true,*
*A blessing for me and you.*
*I hear the rain.*

*Yet through my window it doesn't appear*
*That the rain will ever stop,*
*Still my hope remains sincere*
*With every single drop.*

*For one day soon the fruits of joy*
*Will spring from the fertile ground,*
*And the goodness of it's presence,*
*Will spread it's self around.*

*And many will know that rain will come*
*For the good of all mankind,*
*And afterwards the brightness*
*Of the Lord will shine.*

**Deuteronomy 11:14 That I will give you the rain of your land in his due season, the first rain and the latter rain.**

Many times there's such a drought in our lives that as our faith holds sure we can begin to smell, feel, and even hear the rain before it begins to fall. Why, because we know it's coming. God's Word says it's coming.

The rain is that which is needed to supply necessary minerals in order to sustain and enable growth in life. Too little rain or too much could be harmful to the growth process. Rain in sufficient amounts and in due season is a necessity. If the rain comes out of season the fruit could be ruined.

So pray ye that the Lord will send forth the rain in due season and that you may apply yourself appropriately to reap that which He has purposed in your life.

## Never Neglect Love

*How many people needed you today,*
*Or took up your time in some small way,*
*How often were you misunderstood,*
*And you'd gladly explain if only you*
*could?*

*The needs of others are more than we're*
*aware,*
*Because we've neglected to take time to*
*care.*
*No wonder it's hard for others to under-*
*stand,*
*For neglect of each other was not part of*
*God's plan.*

*So let each one seek to do his share,*
*That none will find life problems too hard*
*to bear*
*And do away with our reasons for not*
*walking in love*
*That we may receive God's blessings from*
*heaven above.*

## 1 John 3:17 ...how dwelleth the love of God in him?

It's sad to think that in our world today it almost seems right to acquire an abundance of money and material goods, while looking away from what may have to be done in order to get it and without consideration of who you might have to hurt along the way. Lots of money is being made on movies and documentaries profiling the rich and their possessions. Little attention is given to the needs of those who suffer without even the very basic of the necessities of life.

The Bible says how can you, having it within your hands to supply a need of your brother, shut up your bowels of compassion towards him. If you can ignore the needs of your brother this way, can you say you love God, or that you have His love working in you? The Bible further says that we're to love the Lord with all our heart, mind, soul, and strength and to love our neighbor as ourselves. So not only are we to consider our needs but also the needs of those around us.

Jesus died that we might have all that we need in this world even eternal life in the world to come. Is He asking too much for us to consider them for whom He died?

## Still I Travel On

*Though it seemed I'd started right,*
*This road I've traveled far,*
*Mostly through the dark of night,*
*With no glimmer of a star.*

*And as the night turned into dawn,*
*This road I've chosen seems wrong,*
*I await the rising of the sun,*
*And still I travel on.*

*There are many passers-by, I see,*
*Some fallen by the way,*
*And though they bid me come with glee,*
*Their faces seem to say.*

*This road we're on has no end,*
*And its joy has long been gone,*
*If I could but start again,*
*Yet still I travel on.*

## Luke 14:23 ...Go out into the highways and hedges, and compel them to come.

There are many people just going through life with no real sense of direction or meaningful destination. They don't even seem to know how or why they're continuing in the way that they are going. Many blame past losses or hurts on why they choose to continue in a certain way. Others just grope about in the darkness of their lives preferring to just be left alone.

Jesus said we're to go into the highways and the by-ways and compel them to come to the great supper of the Lord. He said we were to go to the blind, the maimed, the halt, and the poor and constrain or force them to come.

He said we were to constrain them because many of them are the rejects of our society. They don't meet our standards for beauty, intellect, popularity, or financially acceptable status. Therefore they're not willing to come into our midst, because we've done such a good job making them feel unwelcome.

So I encourage you that once you've discovered the way you ought to be traveling through Christ, that you take the time to stop along the way and tell others, even compel them, to come with you to the great supper.

## Keep the Faith

*Though the distance seems far that I must*
*go,*
*And the road is so unclear,*
*I'll lift mine eyes to God for I know,*
*That His love will hold me near.*

*Though my paths may curve with hills up*
*high,*
*Or dip beneath the sea.*
*Toward Him my heart will, soon draw*
*nigh.*
*And hope will carry me.*

*One day I'll round the curve toward home,*
*With the strength of a thousand men.*
*I'll hear Him say well done My child,*
*You've endured til the end.*

**2 Timothy 4:7 I have fought a good fight, I have finished my course, I have kept the faith.**

As many opportunities as there are to give up in this world there are an equal amount of opportunities to continue through faith in God. Through faith in God we endure discouragement and hardships designed to snuff out hope and cause us to surrender our lives to the destructive forces of this world.

Overcoming the temptation to give up requires that we resist all forces contrary to God's word be they large or small. Paul compared it to a fight realizing at the end of his life that he had remained faithful to God. The good fight of faith is a spiritual battle that takes place in our minds and spirits. Paul was sure of his faith in God as seen in v. 6, **"for I am now ready to be offered."**

Regardless of what you're going through I encourage you to keep the faith. For God is faithful and He will enable you to finish your course.

## The Things That Bind Us

*It's the joy, the sadness, the happiness,
and sorrows,
Our doubts and fears and our hopes for
tomorrow,
The touching and caring, the giving and
sharing,
The coming together in grief and child
bearing.*

*It's our building up and tearing down,
The things that we sow in common
ground.
Yet most of all it's God's plan from above,
That binds us in Him through the power of
love.*

**Hebrews 13:1,3 Let brotherly love continue. Remember them that are in bonds, as bound with them.**

These Scriptures admonish us to yield ourselves in a compassionate way toward others. Compassion is not only feeling the needs and sufferings of others but it moves to ease the burden of that one in need. It comforts and encourages and goes out of the way to supply that which is needed.

It's important that we don't get too caught up in the busyness of things that we forget the purpose of God's call on our lives. Under-girding each other in the love of God in times of need binds us together making us an unbeatable force to anything that would seek to prevent or destroy us.

## Secrets

*Secrets are those special thoughts,*
*That no one know but you,*
*Those inner hopes, fears, or doubts,*
*That may never ever come true.*

*Secrets are the things we find,*
*So very hard to say,*
*And so we hide them in our hearts,*
*And hope they'll always stay.*

*Yet one day you'll meet someone,*
*And an exchange of thoughts will begin,*
*That's when secrets can build a relation-*
*ship,*
*And bring to you a life-long friend.*

**Proverbs 18:24 A man that hath friends must shew himself friendly: and there is a friend that sticketh closer than a brother.**

God does not expect us to live our lives closed off from those round about us. There are some things that you can't tell some people because of their lack of spiritual growth and inability to handle some things. However having a standoffish, refrigerator-type personality is a problem.

One of the main things that stand out about friends is that they share secrets or intimate information with each other. Jesus is that friend that sticks closer than a brother. You can tell Him any and everything and expect Him to safeguard it for your good. Jesus will advise you about your most confidential matter in order that you govern yourself in a way that is uplifting and becoming to the Gospel.

So it's okay to open up and show yourself friendly to those you meet, knowing that you have a friend that cares for you and will help you in every situation that you're faced with.

## A True Marriage

*Love in marriage few may,*
*Ever come to know,*
*The depth of a union,*
*Far beyond the status quo,*

*Being defined by one,*
*Whom can't begin to explain,*
*How I come to partake,*
*Of the love I now proclaim.*

*I know I sought knowledge,*
*Outside of which I understood,*
*To taste of a love,*
*I never dreamed I ever would.*

*I learned how to give,*
*And receive from His hand,*
*In earnest expectation,*
*Of the Master's marriage plan.*

*That as one we can express,*
*The true image of His love,*
*And bring to life a true marriage,*
*Wrought in the heavens up above.*

## Ephesians 5:22-33

There are many people that go through a marriage ceremony that never really partake of the beauty of a true marriage. A true marriage can only come through the knowledge of God in Christ Jesus.

As the husband takes on his proper role in the marriage through submission to God he learns how to love his wife and receive from her what God has purposed for him through her. He's also able to teach her through love what God has purposed for her. As she submits herself to him she become more open to receive from him and from God.

Scripture says that as the husband expresses his love for his wife through giving himself for her, he's able to cleanse her with the washing of the water by the word, and then he can present her unto himself without spot or wrinkle. He can then expect her to be separated unto himself only. This union is compared in Scripture to the relationship Christ has with the church with the two becoming one.

People may live together for many years but true marriages are in Christ.

## Trust Him

*Look up dear heart, for help's on the way,*
*God's power starts moving the second you*
*pray,*
*Just believe in your heart and you will see,*
*God make your request a reality.*

*Just trust in Him, put your mind at rest,*
*Let God work His plan, He'll give you*
*what's best,*
*To fit your life, and meet every need,*
*While confessions bring life to your faith*
*seed.*

*Now there's one thing that when absent*
*we need,*
*Let your heart be patient, and your mind*
*take heed,*
*Your answer shall come, and this being for*
*sure,*
*With added blessings from heaven to all*
*that endure.*

**Psalm 42:11 Why art thou cast down, Oh my soul? and why art thou disquieted within me? hope thou in God: for I shall yet praise Him, who is the health of my countenance, and my God.**

Are the pressures of the world getting you down? Has the enemy come in like a flood against you? Then look up and hope in God. When Jesus is your portion, when He is supplying your needs, what lack ye? You only need to make your request known to Him, and patiently wait for His answer. Scripture says let patience have it's perfect work that you may be entire wanting nothing.

Also remember that when you make your request make it in accordance with the will of God. For His Word says that if we ask anything according to His will He hears us, and that if He hears us we have that which we ask of Him. That's something to look up about. Knowing that you can trust Him is something to shout about.

So don't let the enemy get you down and discouraged, know that God is with you and that He will hear and answer your prayers.

## Dreams Come to Pass

*Lord take not away the dreams I have,*
*Some now of long ago,*
*Nor let me lose my faith in You,*
*Nor the things I come to know.*

*Each waking moment of my life,*
*Help me pursue Your perfect way,*
*To accomplish to the uttermost,*
*Success within each day.*

*Let mercy and truth preserve me,*
*As I do what I must do,*
*With the presence of Your Spirit,*
*Guiding me the whole way through.*

*Seeing my dreams come to pass,*
*As You told me they would,*
*And every thing in my life,*
*Working for my good.*

## Genesis chapters 37-50

We find throughout these chapters in Genesis that Joseph had had several dreams and he'd made them known to his brothers and his father, which seemed to have been an error.

Now, you know the story how that as soon as Joseph's brothers heard his dreams they began to plot against him, how they might prevent them from coming to pass. However God had a different plan, because if God be for you who or what can be against you. Even though Joseph was thrown into a ditch to die by his brothers, and was taken out and sold into slavery instead and even after being thrown into prison on false charges, his dreams still came to pass. God worked it all out for his good. What his brothers meant for harm, what they thought would prevent him, God turned it around and used it to the good of His plan and purpose for Joseph.

God is working the same in your life. It may look like it's all over and that nothing's going to work out for you, but if you'll humble yourself and work as unto the Lord, wherever you are God will raise you up, and bring your dreams to pass just as He has spoken it to you. Dreams do come to pass.

## A Disciple's Prayer

*I weep for the souls of the people dear*
*Lord,*
*For they know not the way to go,*
*They keep not the law of which they've*
*heard,*
*And their hearts run to and fro.*

*I weep for their hurt, their sorrow, and*
*pain*
*For which they know not why,*
*I pray You reveal Your love to them,*
*That in You they may rely.*

*That they seek You in sincerity,*
*That in truth they may learn,*
*That in faith they might believe,*
*And to You their hearts return.*

**2 Corinthians 5:18 And all things are of God, who has reconciled us to Himself by Christ Jesus, And hath given to us the ministry of Reconciliation;**

There is a very real burden for the lost in the hearts of those that love God. Having been brought back into fellowship with the Father through Jesus, we want to see others return as well. However there are those whom after having received the Lord in their lives have not committed themselves to the ministry of reconciling others unto Him.

Jesus said the harvest is great but the laborers are few. Then He said pray ye the Lord of the harvest will send forth laborers.

When you begin to walk in the love of God in sincerity, you'll have real compassion for those suffering with the entanglements of sin in their lives. You'll say with all honesty, "here am I Lord send me." The word of reconciliation will be in you like a burning fire shut up in your bones and many will be reconciled to Christ. I pray you will yield yourself to be so used of God.

## Making the Right Choices

*Have you ever needed direction,*
*A plain simple way to go,*
*And when you asked those around you,*
*None of them seemed to know,*
*Now I had heard from many,*
*How difficult the going could get,*
*And as I told my friends my problems,*
*They'd say you ain't seen nothing yet.*

*So I turned to the God of wisdom,*
*And told Him of my troubled way,*
*He embraced me with arms of love,*
*As He began to say,*
*There's a way that seems right my child,*
*Go not in the direction there of,*
*For its wisdom is not drawn,*
*On the knowledge from above,*

*And the crowd that beckons you to follow,*
*Never ever turn therein,*
*For their paths have taken hold of,*
*A game they cannot win.*
*But there is a narrow path,*

*Very few are willing to take,*
*For it offers simple choices,*
*That you must be willing to make.*

*God's life or the way you've been,*
*God's wisdom or that of men,*
*His Holy Spirit to take control,*
*Or continue the way that you've been told.*
*Sincerity in love or dishonesty and deceit,*
*Victory in Christ or doubt and defeat,*
*Choose you this day is your God-given*
*right,*
*For the choices you make, will determine*
*your plight.*

**Deuteronomy 30:19 ... that I have sat before you life and death, blessing and cursing: therefore choose life, that both thou and thy seed may live.**

Out of all the things that God could have placed in our control, He gave us the power of choice. We have freedom of choice. Adam and Eve were told that they could choose fruit from all the other trees in the garden but they were not to take fruit from the tree of the knowledge of good and evil. They were also told of the consequences of taking fruit from the wrong tree.

Their choice was to believe God and do as He'd said or to not believe Him and therefore disobey what He'd commanded.

Now we all know the story of how Eve chose not to obey God, being deceived by the serpent. Therefore the plan of salvation, which was purposed before the foundations of the world, was implemented.

Now the same spirit of deception is working in the earth today, only it has gained momentum through the multitude of those who carry the message of deception, being themselves deceived. Yet the choices are the same to choose God and obey His Word, receive the gift of eternal life or choose to obey the serpent where sin doth abide and receive the wages of death. It's up to you to make the right choice.

## He's Never Late

*While waking up to start my day,*
*I'm looking all about,*
*The Master of the universe,*
*Has my schedule all laid out.*

*Even the very thoughts I have,*
*Are suggestive of His love,*
*One thing leads to another,*
*With its orders from above.*

*I hurry to finish early*
*Though I know I never should,*
*And errors of my hastiness,*
*Seem to serve me good.*

*And when I've really blown it,*
*Having made a total mess,*
*God's grace comes in on time,*
*Giving me His very best.*

**Ecclesiastes 3:1 To everything there is a season, and a time to every purpose under heaven.**

God is in complete control of what's going on in our lives. If He's in control He has to be aware of our every endeavor. He knows the times and dates of our deadlines. He knows our wedding dates, when our bills are due or when foreclosures are threatened. He knows when the baby's due and when school starts, about job lay offs, hospital bills, and cost for college. He knows when the boss is unfair, when pressures building up, and that you're at your wits end. God knows all these things and so very much more.

He knew we needed a Savior therefore He sent forth Jesus, the sum total of His grace towards us, that through Him all our needs would be met.

God loves us and is always looking for the time whereby He may intervene in our lives to fulfill His promises to us of an abundant life. How can He ever be late, He created time. He's not governed by time, time is governed by Him. He is never late!

## The Road to the Cross

*Shackled by fear in unseen pain,*
*My heart being so distressed,*
*Along with my hurt, I sought God again,*
*And with many tears confessed.*

*Yet it was not easy that I found my way here,*
*Many times I would lose my way,*
*But now with joy unspeakable,*
*At the Cross of Jesus I lay.*

*At the Cross I find strength divine,*
*And peace to carry me through,*
*Now in my heart His Spirit abides,*
*And there's room at the Cross for you.*

**Matthew 16:24 If any man will come after me, let him deny himself, and take up his cross, and follow me.**

The Scripture points out the need for complete surrender of oneself to the obedience of the Word of God, which calls for us to live a crucified life. There are those who will follow Him afar off but are not willing to be crucified with Him.

The decision we make for salvation is not just to escape the flames of hell but, we agree to do even as He did and that is, sacrifice our lives here in the earth, and let Him live His life through us.

There are many altar calls given every Sunday and at big crusade meetings however you never hear the minister say, like Jesus said to His followers, to paraphrase, now remember when I give the altar call and you come forth it means you're willing to deny your self and live a crucified life until you die. Because if such an altar call was given I don't think we'd see very many people coming forth.

Scripture says that we are to present our bodies a living sacrifice and that this is our reasonable service. So when we find our way to the Cross through whatever measures necessary to get us there, many times it's there when we realize it's where we should have been long before.

## Bound By His Blood

*We were drawn by a force,*
*Our hearts could not withstand,*
*And given each our part,*
*According to the Master's plan.*

*He said we were to labor,*
*Eternal life would be our pay,*
*As we tell the whole wide world,*
*That Jesus Christ is the way.*

*Love me with all your heart he said,*
*And my word always give heed,*
*And when they see you love each other,*
*You'll be my disciples indeed.*

*Now we are bound by His blood,*
*To love each other as He said,*
*For when we refuse to love each other,*
*We make vain the blood He shed.*

## John 3:16; 1 John 3:23

Because of the awesome love that God had towards us, He gave His son Jesus to die on the Cross for us, that through His death and the shedding of the blood of the sinless Son, of God, we might be saved. By us believing that Jesus died, was buried, and rose from the dead, and allowing Him to live His life through us, by being obedient to His word, we show forth His love.

There's a lot that could be said in regard to being obedient to His Word, but the Scripture said it all in I John 3:23 that we should believe on Jesus, the Son of God and love one another as He gave commandment. Just as we are obligated to obey the Word of God we are also obligated to walk in love towards each other. To deny one is to deny the other. If the one does not exist then the other does not exist. So I admonish you brethren to love ye one another as He gave commandment, that His shed blood be not in vain.

## Where's the Proof

*Prove to me His love's not real,*
*And these words I speak aren't true,*
*Tell me you don't even feel,*
*The love God has for you.*
*When the pains of sin are strong,*
*And relief you cannot find,*
*Prove to me the love of God,*
*Doesn't even cross your mind.*

*Prove to me He heard not your cry,*
*Even though you did not speak,*
*Tell me you didn't even sigh,*
*And your heart did not feel weak.*
*When your friends have turned away,*
*And there's no one to be found,*
*Prove to me the word of God,*
*Is not a comforting sound.*

*Prove to me I've not been saved,*
*From evil which had me bound,*
*Tell me the love God gracefully gave,*
*Doesn't bring walls of evil down.*
*When I reached out to Him for rest,*
*From the world, and for victory,*
*Prove to me that happiness,*
*Is not knowing He lives in me.*

**2 Corinthians 5:17 Therefore if any man be in Christ, he is a new creature: old things are passed away, behold, all things are become new.**

There are many in the world today who would like to receive a sign that God/Jesus is real. Some are even searching for materialistic proof of His existence. There are confessed atheist and many other non-believers that just go about living their lives as though there is no God. I'd like to say to the non-believers, prove to me that He doesn't exist.

Now those of us that know Him know that we received Him by faith, and after having believed on Him things began to happen in our lives that made us know that He was real. Changes began to take place on the inside of us. Our desire changed, our thoughts changed, our speech changed, and our actions changed. The word of God made us over again. Our old image, inside and out, passed away and everything was made new, and the course of our lives would never be the same.

Where's the proof? It's within me and not just me only but in everyone who believes.

### Faith in God's Word

*I know not where I'm going*
*But I'm determined to trust His choice*
*For there's a wonderful assurance,*
*In the comfort of His voice.*

*His authority and power,*
*With revelations of the end,*
*Is enough to keep me going*
*When it seems that I can't win*

*I believe in His promise*
*Of a home eternally*
*With the God of my salvation*
*That's where His Word is leading me.*

**Matthew 8:8 The centurion answered and said, Lord, I am not worthy that thou shouldest come under my roof: but speak the word only, and my servant shall be healed.**

There is power and authority in the Word of God and this authority was recognized by the centurion. He undoubtedly had seen how that when Jesus spoke, things happened. As he thought about the authority he had and that he himself was under, he began to put it together concerning Jesus and the word. He, knowing that when he gave his servants orders that they obeyed him, therefore seeing that when Jesus spoke, the word obeyed Him, he knew he could say to Jesus "send the word only."

The Word of God is true and everlasting. Scripture says heaven and earth would pass away but the Word would never pass away, but that it all would be fulfilled. It says in Proverbs that the word is life to them that find it and health to all their flesh. Matt 4:4 says **man shall not live by bread alone, but by every word that proceedeth out of the mouth of God.**

So committing yourself to faith in the Word of God should be easy, for in it we have life.

### God's Grace Is Sufficient

*A storm is coming as seen ahead,*
*Dark clouds are rolling in.*
*I know not where it is bound,*
*Nor how soon it might end.*

*Storms are frequent in the springtime,*
*When dreams of life are high.*
*Suddenly the winds of discouragement will*
*rise,*
*To cause all hope to die.*

*But He who controls the winds and the*
*rain,*
*The sunshine and fruitfulness too.*
*Is able to cause all grace to abound,*
*In abundance toward me and you.*

**2 Corinthians 12:9 My grace is sufficient for thee: for my strength is made perfect in weakness.**

Because we are made of flesh and have reasonability, there are times when the trials and storms of life cause us to focus too much on our inabilities. As with Paul, God may not choose to remove the situation, but may expect you to simply trust Him.

In realizing your weakness you are constantly aware of your need for Christ's intervention in the affairs of your life. Also with your awareness you escape the temptation of becoming dependent on self.

If you are experiencing some trouble in your life and you think that you lack the ability to resolve the problem, you are just right for Christ. His grace is sufficient, for when you are weak then are you made strong through Christ.

## He's A God You Can Trust

*Does God really know,*
*The inner pain in which you bare,*
*Does He know when you are hurting,*
*And that no one seems to care?*

*Does He hear the prayers of your heart,*
*Or see the tears that you cry,*
*Does He know the path you're walking*
*When you don't even know why?*

*There's something about trust,*
*That I'm beginning to see,*
*As I acknowledge God's presence,*
*The road ahead is clear to me.*

*Trust in Him is not a matter,*
*Of making sure He does things right,*
*But it's believing He will do it,*
*When there's no possible way in sight.*

*So go ahead and talk to God,*
*Confide in Him all you must,*
*For He's a God that will answer,*
*He's a God that you can trust.*

**Hebrews 4:15 For we have not a high priest which cannot be touched with the feelings of our infirmities; but was in all points tempted like as we are, yet without sin**

The very fact that God, through His Word, took on the housing of a man, even the man Jesus Christ, and was in all points tempted as we are, puts Him in touch with our feelings and thus moves Him to extend Himself mercifully to change our situations for the good.

Knowing that God understands and feels our pain, hurts, and sorrows we can come to Him in the worst of situations. Without fear we can make known to Him the depths of our petitions knowing that He will lovingly consider our needs and answer us accordingly. We can trust Him, for He will answer.

## Joy Unspeakable

*Just knowing that you've brought a smile,*
*To someone suffering with pain,*
*The building of hope in one's life,*
*Is as the sunshine after the rain.*

*Quiet moments with loved ones safety*
*from foes,*
*An inner calm of surety and peace,*
*The gladness of knowing all answers are*
*yours,*
*From knowledge that never will cease,*

*A relationship true to the heart,*
*And binding through out all time,*
*The greatness of God and His glory,*
*With the knowledge that Jesus is mine.*

**1 Peter 1:8 ....ye rejoice with joy unspeakable and full of glory.**

The knowledge of who God is, with His love, His abilities, and His purposes for man, produces an overwhelming joy which can not be adequately explained with just mere words. The affects of just His presence in our lives is mind-boggling, not to mention His interventions, the number of which we can't begin to give an account of nor measure the degree of each one's affect in our lives.

As we allow ourselves to meditate on Him through the many varying experiences that we face of heaviness, temptations, and the numerous sufferings, through faith in Him as our salvation, we will begin to rejoice with a joy that's unspeakable and full of glory.

## The Saving Power of Love

*Someone's calling out while drowning in
pain,
And fear from deep within,
And reaching out not knowing why,
For the help of helpless men.*

*Sometimes in pain you are tossed to and
fro,
Not knowing which way to go,
As you call out to God, with all your
heart,
A Light will begin to show.*

*The shadows of things, which brought you
fear,
Will disappear like clouds in the wind,
And the hand of God will reach out to
you,
And His love will reel you in.*

**Jeremiah 33:3 Call unto me, and 1 will answer thee, and shew thee great and mighty things, which thou knowest not.**

Here the Lord God is talking to the prophet Jeremiah while he is in prison, and his countrymen are in captivity after having had many casualties of war. God is saying, "Call upon me and I will answer." Then He says not only will I answer, but I'll show you great and mighty things, that you don't know.

Now this was just what Jeremiah needed to hear. Being in prison he had to think that there was nothing he could do about his own personal condition, not to mention the condition of his country and fellow citizens.

Maybe you're going through a crisis right now or maybe a financial situation or health issues have you in over your head. If you don't know what to do, where to turn, or how to get out of the difficulties in your life, then listen quietly for His voice...Call unto me and I will answer thee and show you great and mighty things which thou knowest not.

## The Coming of the Lord Is Nigh

*The season is nearing,*
*The signs of the time,*
*Jesus said the end would be.*

*Love has waxed cold,*
*Salvation's being sold,*
*The world's full of misery.*

*Trials in the earth are getting stronger,*
*Foundations being shaken and tossed,*
*Empires that reached up to the sky*
*Are taking a terrible loss.*

*Announcements of marriages*
*Are being advertised,*
*Divorce is at an all time high,*

*Husbands don't know,*
*Why their wives are upset,*
*And the wives refuse to say why.*

*This message comes with encouragement,*
*To all you who believe,*

*Abide in the truth of God's Word,*
*And let not your heart be deceived.*

*He's coming again just as He said,*
*To receive us up above,*
*And eternally in the heaven's*
*We shall abide in the Father's love.*

**Matthew 24:3, 4-51 ...the disciples came unto Him privately, saying, Tell us, when shall these things be? and what shall be the sign of thy coming, and of the end of the world?**

We find the disciples here questioning Jesus about certain things that He had said would be coming upon the earth. They wanted to know when can they expect it to happen and what signs should they be looking for.

They might have been thinking when should they prepare for what was to come. However Jesus warns them in v. 44 that they should always be ready, saying ... **for in such an hour as you think not the Son of man cometh.**

Jesus said they were to watch and in v. 37 He said ...**as the days of Noe were, so shall also the coming of the Son of man be.**

There are many signs given of the end time in Matt 24. It's important to read this chapter for you'll see that many of the signs have already been fulfilled and that Jesus can come at any time. So I admonish you to be ready.

## Lord Never Let Me Be Afraid

*Let me never be afraid*
*Of the way that leads to life,*
*Nor to follow the paths of peace*
*Where there's no pain or strife.*

*Let not the fears of others*
*Keep me from reaching out,*
*Nor let their stories of defeat*
*Ever cause me to doubt.*

*In these times of failing answers*
*Where every reason seems okay,*
*Let me never speak anything*
*You've not told me to say.*

*Let me always hope to see*
*What my heart knows to be true,*
*That on the other side of this life*
*Is eternal life with You.*

**2 Timothy 1:7 For God hath not given us the spirit of fear; but of power, and of love, and of a sound mind.**

Many times people are hindered from serving God by their fear of criticism. They fear what may be the affects of a particular behavior that the Word of God may be requiring of them. Fear may even cause some to hold on to a certain life style thus avoiding criticism and persecution.

Scripture says that "if you be ashamed of Me before men, I'll be ashamed of you before My Father in heaven." Many times holding on to a certain life style apart from God creates an unrealistic and deceptive type life, which produces pride and a lack of true values.

The Word says that if any man will come after Me let him deny himself take up his cross and follow Me. When the enemy has a person so deceived that he withholds complete surrender of himself, he may only have an interest in God, but doesn't really know God, therefore many anxieties and fears will manifest themselves in his life. So then it's imperative to get to know Him in order to rid ourselves of the fear of the lies of the enemy.

God love us and watches over us. He has charged His angels to encamp around us. He has promised us an abundant life and has said He will never leave us nor forsake us. We can rest in Him, rolling all our cares upon Him for He cares for us.

### The Anticipation of Redemption

*One day I'll leave this world of sorrow,*
*To go to that new world of tomorrow.*
*Where upon no face will sadness be,*
*There will be no tears, no pain, and no*
*misery.*

*Where joy will fill the whole establishment*
*And everyone I meet will be heaven sent*
*But until that day comes, and it's coming*
*for sure*
*I'll rest in His love, and in His love I'll*
*endure.*

**Revelation 21:4 And God shall wipe away all tears from their eyes; and there shall be no more death, neither sorrow, nor crying, neither shall there be any more pain: for the former things are passed away.**

It's good to know that in the midst of all the difficulties of this present world, God has a plan of redemption that gives us hope for a life with Him free from pain and sorrow. Scripture says many are the afflictions of the righteous but God delivers him out of them all. So even though we go through things in this world we can hope to be delivered even while we yet live. But one day we're going to be with Him in that place that Scripture says He's gone to prepare for us. There'll be no more crying, no death, no sorrow, no pain, for the former things are passed away. All those things that produced the hurt within us will be done away with. Praise the Lord!

## There's an Appointed Time

*It's appointed unto every man*
*A day and time to die,*
*On which his deeds in this old world*
*God's judgment will rely.*

*Things he hoped to do,*
*Many of which are left half done,*
*And those of highest value,*
*Were never even begun.*

*If only we had more time*
*To realize our days are few,*
*Then maybe while we're able*
*We'd do all that we could do.*

*Oh God, stir up our hearts,*
*Rekindle desire, strength, and love,*
*Replace the ruin in our life,*
*With prosperous works from above.*

*So when that great day comes,*
*And we stand before Thy judgment seat,*
*We will offer deeds of love,*
*And our life in You complete.*

**Hebrews 9:27 And as it is appointed unto men once to die, but after this the judgment.**

The Scripture serves as a warning or even as a type of exhortation to live your life in such a way that you will receive a favorable judgment after death. Also, even though the Scripture doesn't speak of the specific rewards or penalties to be assigned in this particular passage, yet it's very clear that this event of judgment will take place.

I don't believe that God is going to be so much concerned with how or why you did some things, rather more with the nature of your character, the intent of your heart, did you walk in love and seek to lift Jesus up in all that you did, and did you love your neighbor as yourself?

I believe the Scripture supports me in that if you govern your life in the light of what's stated above, you can rejoice when you stand before God on the day of judgment.

### The Gift of God

*God didn't mean that life's events,*
*Should ever force your way,*
*But that you'd seek His face,*
*In each and everyday.*

*God didn't plan for man,*
*To act out of fear,*
*But in boldness of faith,*
*As His voice you hear.*

*God didn't plan that any man,*
*Should ever fall*
*Or loose his way,*
*Or ignore His call.*

*His plan is written and plain to see,*
*When proclaimed by those who've been set*
*free,*
*It's eternal life He wants you to receive,*
*For it's God's gift to all that believe.*

**Isaiah 9:6 For unto us a child is born, unto us a Son is given: and the government shall be upon His shoulders: and His name shall be called Wonderful, Counsellor, The mighty God, The everlasting Father, The Prince of Peace.**

This Scripture points out the abundant awesome love that God has toward man in that the Child was born but the Son was given. Jesus was given that we might live. Scripture says that God gave Him that we should not perish but have everlasting life.

There is no other name on earth whereby we might be saved and there is no way whereby we might earn salvation, it is the gift of God. So all we have to do is believe on the name of the Lord Jesus, that He is the Son, of God, that He died and rose again from the dead, and you shall be saved. The gift of God is a Person, even the Lord Jesus Christ. God gave Him, we only have to receive Him.

### God's Miracle of Love

*Congratulations on your decision,*
*To walk in unity,*
*To enter plans in life ahead,*
*As both your hearts agree.*

*To face the trial's of life,*
*With God's wisdom as your guide,*
*Through faith in love and righteousness*
*As you've promised to abide.*

*To honor all mankind,*
*With the gifts God's given you,*
*As you purpose in your heart to do,*
*All the things He tells you to.*

*Never to leave each other,*
*Nor forsake your vows of love,*
*In this I know you shall remain together,*
*And receive God's blessings from above.*

**Ephesians 5:31 ... and they two shall be one flesh.**

God is love (1 John 4:8) and the miracle of that love is when man allows God to shed that love abroad in his heart so completely to when through submission to God, he can be made one with another.

The statement of the vows in marriage doesn't make the two one, it's the acknowledgment and obedience to the Word of God that makes them one.

When two people are drawn together with a desire toward love, wanting to know each other so deeply and so completely that they choose to commit to each other in marriage, they're saying to God "we are desirous to be made one with each other, make us one." And the miracle work of God begins.

## True Love

*Precious are the moments,*
*That's most seldom spoken of,*
*Where in are defined deep,*
*Expressions of our love.*

*Frequent are the gentle,*
*Loving smiles on your face,*
*Sending unspoken signals,*
*Of a love pure and safe.*

*The visits with true friends,*
*As days quickly turn to years,*
*Where treasured memories,*
*Have replaced all our fears.*

*I once asked God,*
*If true love could ever be,*
*And I knew His answer was yes,*
*When He gave you to me.*

## Ephesians 5:25, 22

The best example of true love in the Scriptures is Jesus dying on the Cross for man. God so loved the world that He gave Jesus to die for us. Yet we find Jesus, during the time leading up to His crucifixion saying, "no man take my life, I lay it down." When Peter pulled his sword and cut off the ear of the soldier, Jesus put the ear back on and said don't you know I can pray the Father and He shall presently give me twelve legions of angels?

Jesus loved the church and showed forth the example of a sinless life. Even so is the husband to love his wife and show forth the example of Christ before her. The wife then is to submit herself to her husband as unto the Lord. In this we see the most precise example of true love.

## Blue Skies

*I believe there's blue*
*Behind every cloud,*
*And enough joy,*
*To make you shout out loud.*

*No pain or sorrow*
*Can last always,*
*There's always happier,*
*And brighter days.*

*So regardless the difficulty,*
*Or the trial you go through,*
*There's always something,*
*That you can do.*

*Begin to look up,*
*With every cloud anew*
*And see behind each one,*
*God's sky of blue.*

**Psalm 34:19 Many are the afflictions of the righteous: but the Lord delivereth him out of them all.**

In the process of becoming renewed in Christ we experience many trying and hurtful moments. In times past we'd do all we could to avoid most of these experiences, however in time we've learned that it's important that we go through them for the purpose of renewal. Our resistance and our avoidance of things should have to do with our refusal to continue as we were.

The pain and sorrow of the afflictions we must experience are very real and if there were another way of us acquiring the renewal that we need, we'd gladly take it up. But praise be to God we have the promise of the Word that though there will be many afflictions, He will deliver us out of them all.

Yes there are some cloudy days and maybe even some stormy nights, but storms don't last always, the sun will shine again. Weeping may endure for a night but joy cometh in the morning.

## The Need for Complete Surrender

*Looking out my window I see,*
*Many possibilities,*
*So many avenues leading away,*
*From my pain.*
*I see and smell the fragrance,*
*Of accomplishment,*
*The odor of renewal, desire*
*And gain.*

*God has placed deep within us,*
*A vein of potential,*
*An abundance of ability,*
*To tap out the gold,*
*Through the power of His Spirit,*
*We'll reach our potential,*
*Through complete surrender to Him*
*Of our heart, mind, and soul.*

**Hebrews 10:38 ... If any man draw back, my soul shall have no pleasure in him.**

There's a well accepted mentality that we are totally dependent upon ourselves, therefore turning the responsibility for our lives over to someone else is very hard, even next to impossible when that someone else is God. Even those who are confessed Christians will say things like "God helps those who help themselves" or "God expects you to use your common sense." These statements however couldn't be further from the truth. In fact, God says that you are to lean not to your own understanding, and that in all your ways you are to acknowledge Him. He wants to care for you, to direct your ways, to order your footsteps. He wants you to renew your mind, to be not conformed to the ways of this world, but to be transformed.

Transformation can only take place through complete surrender of your heart mind, soul, and strength to God through Jesus Christ as your Lord and Savior. Then and only then can you receive the power of God to reach your potential.

## The Director

The director nodded to the musicians,
It was time to play a new song.
He motioned to the choir before him,
Their positioning was wrong.

They quickly moved as in rhythm,
Like that of a marching band,
Their mouths all fell open,
At the lifting of his hand.

How precious is the music,
When we can make a choice,
To send forth words of beauty,
As though singing with one voice.

Each one paying attention,
To the part he must sing,
While delighting in the hope,
Of the joy his song can bring.

What music you can make,
When directed by His will,
To say and do things,
Not by how you think or feel.

But if in His righteousness,
You purpose your heart to act in love,
You'll find that God's own Spirit,
Will direct you from above.

### Romans 8:14 For as many as are led by the Spirit of God, they are the sons of God.

Scripture says that to as many as received Him to them gave He power to become the sons of God even to them that believed on His name. Now here in Romans it says as many as are led by the Spirit, they are the sons of God. This is saying that you can have the Spirit and yet not be led by the Spirit. It's saying that being led by the Spirit is up to you. You can hear the voice of God speaking to you and still choose to do your own thing or you can obey His voice. We need to submit ourselves to obey His voice and allow Him to guide us through life's events.

Life is so much more complicated than much of the superficial aspects that we try to deal with on our own. Even those who think themselves to be super intelligent don't come anywhere close to conquering the real problems of this world, which is sin.

God has dealt with sin through the death of His only begotten Son on the Cross. Jesus conquered sin for us and all we have to do is accept His finished work and let Him direct our lives by His Spirit dwelling inside of us.

If you love God and have accepted His Son Jesus as Lord of your life, you can ask Him for the Holy Spirit to come and live on the inside of you that you may be directed by the Spirit of God till Jesus returns and He will give Him to you. Just ask in faith just as you did for your salvation and He will give Him to you. Amen.

## Remember The Red, White, and Blue

*Remember the red for the blood that was
shed,
The white, which covered our dead,
The blue broken hearts for those which
were lost,
The widows, which now hang their heads.*

*Remember the things, which make us one,
Hope in liberty, our country, and love,
The battles we won through sacrifice of
our sons
And the shedding of innocent blood.*

*Remember Christ died to make men free
He did it for me and for you,
So in troubled times I know that God,
Remembers the red, white, and blue.*

## Genesis chapter 9

God made man in His image and in His likeness and breathed His very life into him instructing him to go and be fruitful. Any thing and anybody that takes away the life of man, which is in the blood, God will require it of him. Even in the time of the anguish of God toward man, where He had allowed flood waters to destroy man, except for Noah and his family, God, afterwards made a covenant never again to permit the waters to become so great as to destroy all flesh. He sealed the covenant He made with man with the rainbow of distinct colors in the clouds as a token of that promise.

Our flag is a representation of the promises of every citizen of the United States in the fear of God to take a stand and even die if need be in the defense of life and liberty for every man in this nation. It was determined that we should remain, an indivisible nation under God. In doing this we submitted and committed our whole nation to God and therefore God committed Himself to us. Along with His commitment to us came His power to keep us a free nation.

So whenever there are threats against this nation, whenever there is war and or loss of life, I know God remembers our commitment to Him, but above this He remembers His commitment to us.

## He's Real

*Did this world just happen,*
*Or is there a real God out there?*
*Does He really listen,*
*And does He really care?*

*Can we call Him in the morning,*
*On a day we fear to see?*
*I'm glad I know that there's a God,*
*That really cares for me.*

*Now some say He's a crutch,*
*In the back of my mind,*
*And some say He's my weakness,*
*That's just giving off its sign.*

*Yet I know that He's my Father.*
*Yes, the living God's my friend,*
*And I dare not trust another,*
*I'll go with Jesus til the end.*

*No, I dare not trust another,*
*I'll go with Jesus til the end.*

**Hebrews 10:23 Let us hold fast the profession of our faith without wavering; (for He is faithful that promised).**

The question of whether God is real has been asked in the hearts and minds of every one of us of reasonable age. This question is also answered in our hearts and minds based on what we choose to believe about Him.

Information about God usually comes to us first from our parents then as we get older we will either seek more information or it will seek us out through others. However you receive the knowledge of God or the Lord Jesus, it's up to you to either believe it or reject it. You can't get around this, because your confession and your actions will be a testament of your beliefs.

However once you believe, it's up to you to hold fast your profession of faith in Him. Your faith will be continually challenged by the influences of principalities and powers, by spiritual wickedness in high places, and through those who don't believe. If we hold fast our faith and refuse to question our own beliefs and standards, rather if we resist those challenges, we will find that He is real through our own witness of His interventions and blessings in our lives.

### A Birthday Wish

*I wish you happiness at all times,*
*But even more today,*
*And that the best of all God has,*
*Will always come your way.*

*I pray that every step you take,*
*Follows God's path and will,*
*To avenues of peace and joy,*
*That only love can give.*

*And on this special day,*
*I wish above all things,*
*That you know my love for you,*
*And the joy that your love brings.*

**Hebrews 13:1 Let brotherly love continue.**

For someone to go out of the way to show love or to do an act of kindness towards someone is not a common practice today. Even in those relationships where we expect to see acts of kindness and love being expressed we don't see it enough. Family relationships are very cold and very strained to say the least. However when the writer said let brotherly love continue he wasn't talking to the family, he was talking to believers.

There is no other place whereby brotherly love should be seen more than in the church, among those who say they walk in His love. The writer is admonishing us to resist temptations that try to cause us not to show forth God's love towards each other, and in so doing we help each other experience more of His joy and peace.

## A Gift of Love

*I love you more than you could ever know,*
*Or that I could think or say,*
*Because my love for you grows deeper,*
*With every passing day.*

*As the knowledge of love provide me with,*
*Opportunities to give,*
*I wrap them in warm thoughts of you,*
*Wherein my heart doth live.*

*And on this special day,*
*May I present you with more love,*
*Drawn on the banks of heaven,*
*From the throne of God above.*

**Ephesians 3:19 And to know the love of Christ, which passeth knowledge, that ye might be filled with all the fullness of God.**

My husband once preached a message on love that I've never forgotten, it just blew me away. He described some of the loose ways most people use the words "I love you." Then he began to talk about the phileo type of love. This type of love would best describe the love a person might have for a friend or a family member, like a child. He also spoke about the eros type of love, which is the type of love a man might have for a woman. The definitions of these types of love, biblical scholars of the days before Christ had no problem communicating to others, but they were unable to give an acceptable definition for agape love. They had nothing whereby they might compare or demonstrate agape love, so my husband said they placed it on the shelf.

However when Jesus came on the scene and began to teach and demonstrate His love, when He taught that we're to love our enemies, do good to them that hate you, bless them that curse you, and pray for those that despitefully use you and persecute you, he said they took the word agape off the shelf and placed it by Jesus. Jesus demonstrated agape love. Yet at the end of Paul's ministry he still wrote of his hope for the Gentiles that God might grant them to know the love of God which passeth knowledge.

Jesus, laying down His life for us is beyond our ability to fully understand. Yet when we allow Him to live His life through us we too become capable of showing an unbelievable capacity to express love. As we draw the knowledge of love from Him who is love, there's no limit. I pray you yield yourself to be a gift of love to someone.

## Christmas Time

*When snow falls gently*
*On a cold winter's night,*
*And stars in the distance*
*Cast a glimmer of light,*
*When fireplace crackles*
*With flames so bright,*
*It's Christmas time to me.*

*When children's laughter*
*Fills the air,*
*And the sounds of music*
*Is everywhere,*
*When friends and family gather near,*
*It's Christmas time to me.*

*Christmas comes but once a year,*
*Bringing love, joy, and plenty of cheer,*
*And though it's gone in a day or two,*
*It's spirit lasts the whole year through.*

## Luke 2:7-20

The sounds of laughter and an aura of joy and cheer are wonderful occurrences that many expect to experience around Christmas time. The celebration of the birth of Christ on Dec. 25th each year has become a tradition in about 80% of the homes of Americans. You can feel the spirit of preparation for the celebrations and hear the abundance of laughter in the air.

Much of the celebrating and partying, which takes place doesn't really have very much to do with any real acknowledgement that it's in recognition of His birthday. Yet the anticipation of the laughter, and cheer with the gathering of family and friends is there anyway. However, in just a few days all of the to do is over and many that don't know Him are left with feelings of anxiety, loneliness, depression, and even of suicide.

Though the day may be gone, the spirit with it's love, joy, and peace don't have to be. Through accepting Jesus into your heart as your Lord and Savior, the love, joy, and peace will not only remain throughout the year, but it will last a lifetime. Just confess your sins, ask His forgiveness, acknowledge that He is the Son of God who came to die on the Cross for our sins and rose again on the third day and you can be saved. God will forgive you, cleanse you, and receive you as His child. I pray you accept Him now. Amen.

### Christmas Is

*Christmas is knowing that there's*
*Someone who cares,*
*And is willing to ease the pain*
*Of the burdens we bear.*

*Christmas is the peace, love, and joy*
*That we feel,*
*And the faith that helps us know*
*That our Savior is real.*

*It's trusting Him who makes us merry,*
*Even when our hearts are blue,*
*It's knowing His love and strength will*
*carry,*
*Us the whole year through.*

**Matthew 1:23 Behold, a virgin shall be with child, and shall bring forth a Son, and they shall call His name Emmanuel, which being interpreted is, God with us.**

The message of Christmas is Emmanuel, God with us. Yes the virgin birth happened and has it's place and value in the way in which the Son of God was to enter this world, but the message of Christmas is God with us. He's not up there somewhere, He's not the man up there, He's not some "higher power," He is God and He is with us.

God seeing the need of man and his fall to sin before the foundations of the world, purposed through His Holy council, to wrapped Himself up in a human suit and through the power of the Holy Ghost entered this world through a virgin, whose named was Mary.

Yes, I'd say He cares; He cared enough to enter into our sufferings bringing with Him the words of life and the value and power of a sinless life, to totally defeat sin, death, and the grave and set free all those who would believe on Him.

It's good to know that He's not a God that is distant and unable to feel our pain, but that He's with us in every area of our lives.

## If Jesus Had Not Been Born

*If Jesus had not been born,*
*The wisemen's journey would have been in*
*vain,*
*And the angels would not have had,*
*Glad tidings to proclaim.*

*The hope of man would have fallen,*
*All debts would be due today,*
*With the cost of his failures being*
*A debt too high to pay.*

*There'd be no Christ in Christmas,*
*There'd be no joy or peace,*
*And all hope for love,*
*Would have suddenly ceased.*

*If Jesus had not been born,*
*Where oh where would I be,*
*I would not know that God,*
*Really cares for me.*

*Fear would have me bound,*
*Doubt and anger would have control,*

*There'd be no way for me,*
*To repossess my soul.*

*His birth was so much more,*
*Than simple words could ever say,*
*It was an everlasting assurance,*
*That everything's okay.*

## Matthew chapter 2

If Jesus had not been born the devastation and the lack would be too much to even describe, because the loss would be far greater than we have the ability to comprehend. First we'd re-enter the place where we were before man first came to know Him. Which means that many of us would have never been born because our fore fathers would not have survived long enough without Him to bring us into the world. There'd be feelings of hopelessness without mercy. The words of love and faith would have no meaning, we'd grope about throughout each day waiting to reap the rewards of worthless living.

To try and imagine a life without Christ

quite frankly is unimaginable for those that know Him. It's even hard for us at times to understand how those that don't know Him manage their lives without Him each day.

To know He lives is to know that everything's okay, that all is well. The holy angels announced it at the birth of Christ, saying **Behold I bring you good tidings of great joy...** glory to God in the highest, peace on earth, and good will toward men. (See Luke 2:10, 14.) All is well!

## A Pillar of Love

*A mother is a pillar in a home of godly love,*
*Distributing messages of truth, and encouragement from above.*

*She sees trouble in the distance, and warns you*
*The way to go, and when you error in your way,*
*She never says I told you so.*

*A mother is wise. And knows just what to do,*
*When the problems are too many, and the Answers are too few.*

*She continues to believe for you, nothing but*
*God's best, and instructs you never to give up,*
*Or settle for less.*

*She cries when you hurt, and rejoices when*

*you win,*
*And when she sees you're giving up, she*
*gets you going again.*
*A mother is someone that no matter where*
*you are*
*The warming presence of her love is never*
*too far.*

**Proverbs 5:19, 31:25**

The woman of God exhibits such inner strength in much of her ways that sometimes it's hard to see her as the weaker vessel spoken of in another part of Scripture. She is continuously planning, watching, doing, and giving of herself in love to her husband, children, neighbors and her community. She is a pillar of strength, which serves to uphold and stabilize the family structure. She has high standards, integrity, and is honorable. She imparts Godly wisdom and love continually and leads her children in paths whereby they may obtain favor from God and safety from all harm. She is to be desired and admired but above these she is blessed and highly favored of God.

## When You Endure

*If you could look through eyes of hope,*
*To see that which you cannot see*
*Or reach to achieve the highest dream,*
*Far beyond your ability.*

*If you could forsake the paths of old,*
*And the speech so common to you,*
*There would be absolutely nothing,*
*Impossible for you to do.*

*God has made a path for us,*
*Words cannot clearly tell,*
*How it reaches beyond the natural,*
*To where the spirit dwells.*

*Where every hope imagined,*
*And every desire unsaid*
*Lie quietly awaiting the call of faith,*
*To raise it from its bed.*

*And when you put your hands to do*
*That which once you were  unsure*
*The evidence of that hope or dream*
*Becomes a gift when you endure.*

### Philippians 4:13 I can do all things through Christ which strengtheneth me.

There's a saying that everything that's worth having is worth fighting for. I don't know about that but I do know that the enemy will try all he can to prevent the things of God from coming to pass in your life. Many times the enemy will try to convince you that God doesn't want you to have whatever it is or that He didn't say what you thought He said about you being able to have or accomplish something. The enemy will even strategize events to discourage your continuance in that thing in which you're hoping for, and sadly to say many times he's successful in getting people to give up.

Paul said in Phil 4:13 **I can do all things through Christ which strengheneth me.** The Word says you have the need of patience after you've done the will of God. God will bring it to pass but we must let patience have its perfect work that we may be entire, wanting nothing.

So endure the hardships like a good soldier only know this, Christ Jesus is your strength. He's begun this good work in you and He will perform it. So, having done all to stand, stand.

### The Road to Holiness

*I woke up on this road one day,*
*Of how I cannot tell,*
*I only know the way I'd go,*
*Was destined sure to fail.*

*While crying to God both day and night,*
*Came strength from I know not where,*
*Sufficient it seemed regardless the load,*
*Or the cross I had to bear.*

*And a sudden burst of knowledge,*
*And a light so bright to me,*
*That every crooked path,*
*Became clear for me to see.*

*Though straight I am to go,*
*In righteousness and in love,*
*I seek Your mantle of holiness,*
*To guide me from above.*

## Luke 11:11-13

In these Scriptures Jesus is speaking to the disciples concerning how to receive the Holy Spirit by asking. Here He says if men knew how to give good gifts how much more would God give the Holy Spirit to them that ask.

In John 16:8 Scripture says when He, the Spirit of truth shall come He will reprove the world of sin and of righteousness. Jesus said that if He didn't go away that the Comforter would not come.

The Spirit of God dwelling on the inside of us is the means whereby God's truths are discerned and separated from the lies of the evil one. It's the means whereby God leads us in the way that we ought to go. It's the way He keeps us from going the wrong way.

Yielding ourselves therefore to receive the Holy Spirit is necessary to assuring that the road we're traveling truly leads to holiness and life eternal with God.

### Encounters of Kindness

*The roads of which we must travel,*
*However far or wide,*
*Are scattered with God's blessings,*
*With His wisdom as our guide.*

*The encounters of one's kindness,*
*Though unsure from the start,*
*Many times end with gladness,*
*As their smiles light up our hearts.*

*As you travel along God's path,*
*Let Him guide you where He may.*
*Knowing He's purposed in every*
*encounter,*
*A special blessing to brighten your way.*

## 2 Kings 4:8; Luke 10:33; Acts 3:6

In each of theses Scripture readings we see encounters of kindness in action. The Shunammite woman in 2 Kings 4:8 didn't have to show forth any kindness to the prophet she just acted on what she believed. There was no indication in previous Scripture that she expected to receive anything from him, only that she sought to show a kindness to a man of God. As a result of this she was blessed tremendously.

The good Samaritan in Luke 10:33 also demonstrated a kindness to the man that fell among thieves. Jesus used this to teach how we ought to be towards our neighbors.

Peter and John in Acts 3:6 could have told the man at the gate that they didn't have any money. This would have been the truth. However they went beyond what he was asking to give the man what he needed which was his hearing.

In each of these encounters the people expressed a kindness purposed by God but given through those who allowed themselves to be so used of God.

He'll use us the same way if we'll yield ourselves to Him.

### Laughter

*A welcome approval of someone or some-*
*thing,*
*A release of inner delight,*
*A contagious expression of the pleasure one*
*brings,*
*That says the moment is special and right.*

*It signals one's mood and opens the door*
*For returning a smile or a word.*
*It varies in size and volume*
*By what has been seen or heard.*

*It's friendly, warm, and full of cheer,*
*And is expressed best when truth prevails.*
*It surrounds us with an aura of desire,*
*By the gloom it dispels.*

**Genesis 21:6 God hath made me to laugh.**

Scripture says to be merry doth good, like medicine. Merriment and fun is conducive to laughter and cheer. More often than not laughter is not spoken of in a good light in Scripture. Not that there's anything wrong with laughter. However you find Scriptures like, your laughter shall be turned into mourning. In proverbs 1:26 **God said I also, will laugh at your calamity.**

Yet we find in Gen 21:6 Sarah saying, **"God hath made me to laugh, so that all that hear will laugh with me."** And she had something to laugh about, something to rejoice about. God had given her a son in her old age whom, had aforetime been barren. God had turned her mourning into laughter. Her spirit was lifted. She could see much good coming out of this. All gloom certainly had been dispelled. Praise God!

## A Free Nation

*Born in the hearts of a people through
hope
Is a place full of common desire.
Where motives and zeal live on every slope
Fueled by ideals with unquenchable fire.*

*Men and women can dare to dream,
And hope for a life of peace.
And partake of the joy that belonging can
bring,
Where true love never ceases.*

*God in our midst as we call on His name,
That united we might stand.
And in one voice we will proclaim,
Freedom for every man.*

**2 Chronicles 7:14 If my people, which are called by my name.**

The hope of the founding fathers of this nation was that we would have a union of the states under one government of standards set forth by the precepts of God as found in the holy Scriptures. It was purposed in the constitution that men would be governed by ideas of righteous living. The idea that somehow the Bible would be observed in the governing of this nation has been in question since the beginning.

Regardless of whether men agree or not, God requires that we acknowledge Him if we're to receive His favor and/or blessings in our lives. We must obey His word, which calls for us to humble ourselves and turn from the ways of evil. He's said in His word that if we will live righteously before Him that He will forgive us and heal our land. That word heal means to get rid of sickness and disease. It means to restore back to health. To heal would be also, to be able to overcome grief, pain, and sorrows, to be free from poverty. In this we see that we need God more today than at any other time in the history of this nation, for many are plagued with the burdens mentioned above.

So I charge each of us to begin to realize the needs of this nation and to humble ourselves turn from our wicked ways and pray, that we might begin to see the healing take place. Then this nation will truly be the free nation that we've hoped for. Amen.

Give the gift of *A Comforting Word*
to your friends, family, and colleagues
**Check your local bookstore
or order here**

[ ] Yes, I want _____ copies of *A Comforting Word
for $9.99 each*

[   ] Yes, I'm interested in having Pastor Wesley
and Alfrenia Gray speak or give a seminar to my
company, association, school, organization or
church. Please send me information.

Include $3.95 for shipping and handling for one
book, and $1.95 for each additional book.
Payment must accompany orders. Allow 3-4
weeks for delivery.

Name_____

Organization_____

Address_____

City/State/Zip_____

Phone_____

Signature_____

**Call (918) 259-5095
Make checks payable and return to:
Brighter Day Greetings
P.O. Box 573
Broken Arrow, OK. 74013-0573**